strong words never heard vol 3

strong words never heard vol 3

lyrics and poetry

peter strong

Strong Words Never Heard, vol 3 © Peter Strong, 2025
All pieces © Peter Built Music ca. 1991–2025
All Rights Reserved.

Paperback ISBN: 978-1-7375267-4-2
eBook ISBN: 978-1-7375267-5-9

Photograph of Peter Strong courtesy of Maxwell Mason

Cover art photo by Nikoline Arns on Unsplash

Editing, formatting, and cover design by
Vicky Haygood Editorial and Book Design Services
www.vickyhaygood.com

To my daughter, Bianca, and my grandchildren, Deandre, Maddux, and Bexley, who ground me in love every day. You are my inspiration!

And to all the artists who use their creativity to make a difference. Thank you!

Contents

To the Reader	1
A Kiss	2
All I Hear	4
All Is Not Lost	6
An Honest Lie	8
Are You Sorry	10
Aren't You Glad	12
Back at It	14
Better	16
Better Self	18
Big Dreams in a Small Town	20
Can't Take Back	22
Capture My Heart Slowly	24
Church Boy	26
Come Home (Before It Gets Too Dark)	28
Corvette	30
Couldn't Be Happier	32
Crazy Town II	34
Dear Aneurysm	36
Dollar Store	38
Don't Blame Love	40
Don't Make Me Go There	42
Even If	44
Explain Away	46
For My Heart	48
Friends Only	50
Full Dream Ahead	52
Fun Fact	54
Get It While It's Hot	56
Getting Started	58
Halftime	60
Happy Heart	62
He Watches Me	64
Heard That Story Before	66
I Believe in Us	68
I Could've Handled Things Better	70
I Don't Know How	72

I Found the Secret 74
I Want to Be Happy 76
I'm Going With You 78
In That Line 80
Intuitive 82
Is This a Bad Time 84
It Could Be 86
It Was a Good Day 88
It's Hard to Hate Up Close 90
Karen's Song 92
Katie June 94
Light on Love Heavy on Shame 96
Lonely 98
Love Gets Better 100
Mia 102
Midnight Med 104
More Than Qualified (to Be My Lover) 106
My Heart Wins the Day 108
My Heroes Weren't Perfect 110
My Way of Drinking 112
Not Today, Not Tomorrow, Not Ever 114
On the Hook 116
One More Thing to Worry About 118
Other Side of Last Year 120
Perfect Silence 122
Picks and Shovels 124
Refused 126
Right Where You're Standing 128
Rule of Thumb 130
See Yourself 132
She Runs Really Well 134
She Still Loves Her Shoes 136
She Won't Be Me 138
Somebody Lied 140
Sounds Like Something You'd Say 142
Strings 144
Sweet Sue Anonymous 146

THE FOLLOW-UP VOICE	148
THE WIND	150
THERE'LL ALWAYS BE ANOTHER JOSH	152
THIRD TIME IS NOT A CHARM	154
UP IN HEAVEN	156
VOLUNTEER	158
WE GOT BACK TOGETHER	160
WHERE ARE WE	162
WHY ARE YOU HERE	164
WON'T PUSH MY HEART AROUND	166
YOU MAKE ME DREAM	168
ABOUT PETER STRONG	171

Acknowledgements

I want to thank my family and friends for their loving support, without which, this book would not be. I am humbled and grateful for all the time and energy you have given to me. It is beyond measure.

I want to thank my co-writers who offered their melodies to the following songs. You continue to help me be a better lyricist and poet.

David Scheibner: *Picks and Shovels*

Florence Phillips: *Better*

Scott Wilk: *Capture My Heart Slowly*

TO THE READER

Each of these pieces is a story unto itself. There is no connection other than they are in the same book and in alphabetical order. I encourage you to read them out loud, if you so desire. You may find they resonate well as spoken word. I welcomed these pieces in "whatever form they were born." And I welcome you to enjoy them as well, and I thank you for sharing this experience with me.

A Kiss

A kiss on the cheek
A kiss on the neck
A kiss on the lips
Is what comes next
The first of many
Any last regrets?
'Cause a kiss everywhere
Is what comes next

A kiss in the kitchen
A kiss in the car
A kiss and a kiss
And a kiss at the bar
A kiss with your eyes
That just says it all
Serious PDA
When you hear last call

A kiss on a mission
A kiss with style
A kiss that leaves you
With a damn good smile
The first of many
You'll never forget
'Cause a kiss everywhere
Is what comes next

A kiss in the shadows
That doubles the fun
A kiss and a kiss
Until you come undone
A kiss you can feel
That makes your toes curl
And in your boudoir
It's out of this world

A kiss that delivers
Again and again
A kiss that persists
Until you say when
The first of many
Any last regrets?
'Cause a kiss everywhere
Is what comes next

A kiss on the cheek
A kiss on the neck
A kiss so delish
You're a total wreck
A kiss you can steal
And no one objects
'Cause a kiss everywhere
Is what comes next

All I Hear

All I hear is hang in hang in hang in
It's a rough patch, it's just a lover's spat
You guys have been the perfect match

All I hear is hold on hold on hold on
Lean on your faith and that will keep you strong
But what if I'm right that together we're wrong

I should never be this sad
It should never be this hard
And I'm gambling with my feelings
You so easily disregard
I want the give and take we knew
And the arms that held me close to you
And your heart that always had my back
And everything that goes with that

All I hear is that guilty guilty voice
That whispers, oh well, I have made my choice
But when I'm home alone this is what I know

I should never be this sad
I should never cry this hard
And I betray my own feelings
When I just leave them where they are
I want this wall to fall away
So I can say the things I need to say
I miss the heart that I once found
That can't find its way to me right now

I won't settle for that crippling myth
That when you love you sign up for this

I should never be this sad
It should never be this hard
And I'm gambling with my feelings
You so easily disregard
I want to mend not make an end
And hold you in my arms again
And feel the heart that had my back
And everything that goes with that

The kiss, the love, the real trust
And everything that was truly us

All Is Not Lost

We've been hurt by those who abuse their power
At this very hour
We can express our rage
We can keep bad actors off the stage
We can reveal their deal
To always kneel to their smaller selves
Leaving us in hell

We've been swindled by some whose hearts have grown numb
For almost everyone
But bullies aren't strong
It's just grandiose gone wrong
They're simply desperadoes
That none of us should ever follow
'Cause it's all a show

We're paying the price at a terrible cost
But all is not lost
We can fight back
We can put good back on track
We can decide to toss
The morally horribly bankrupt boss
All is not lost

We've been duped by words in an endless loop
Of me against you
But wars finally end
And evil will fall on its sword again
And together we'll say
It never ever had to be this way
But it can change

Corruption is nothing but a broken cross
But all is not lost
We can fight back
We can put good back on track
We can love at any cost
We can pick up the pieces where we left off
All is not lost

An Honest Lie

You're not saying the thing I know you feel
'Cause it's going to hurt me something real
Just say something else other than goodbye
I don't want the truth, I want an honest lie

Tell me about the good times we've had
Help me brace my heart for something sad
If you're moving on just don't tell me why
I don't want the truth, I want an honest lie

Make up something that I want to hear
Like the problem is you and I'm in the clear
Make up something I'll never believe
That will stop my tears as you go to leave

I can feel our time quickly running out
And I know you're leaving without a doubt
No need to explain or even justify
I don't want the truth, I want an honest lie

Tell me this isn't what I think it is
And you're really not worth any of this
Make up something I'll never believe
That will stop my tears as you go to leave

The wall is growing wide and tall
I'm not asking you to scale it all

Make up something that I want to hear
Like the problem is you and I'm in the clear
I'll take it to heart and take it as true
Just to get through this moment with you

You're not saying the thing I know you feel
'Cause it's going to hurt me something real
But if I was you, I wouldn't even try
I don't want the truth, I want an honest lie

Just say something else other than goodbye
I don't want the truth, I want an honest lie

Are You Sorry

Are you sorry like "please forgive me"
Or are you sorry you ever met me
Are you sorry for your actions
Or are you making a retraction

Windows stay open for only so long
For you to mean what you say
When you say you were wrong
It seems rather clear from the words I hear
That might be an order too tall
Are you sure this is your apology tour
Or are you really not sorry at all

Are you sorry like I'm sorry
That indiscretions keep coming your way
Or are you sorry so so sorry
The truth caught up with you today

You can make mistakes for only so long
When you double the trouble
Then our world has gone wrong
Is it really clear after shots and beers
You would fall for something so small
Are you sorry once more right down to your core
Or are you really not sorry at all

Tomorrow will change, you'll see less of me
But you'll do more of the same, predictably

Windows stay open for only so long
For you to mean what you say
When you say you were wrong
And you're sorry of course and showing remorse
'Cause the curtain is about to fall
And I'm smiling because I am done with this love
And I'm really not sorry at all

Aren't You Glad

I know you don't think the same as I do
But can we agree on some things that are true

Aren't you glad
You got out of bed
Aren't you glad
You took one step ahead
Aren't you glad
Now you feel less sad
Aren't you glad

In spite of troubles that double us down
I want to believe we can gain some ground

Aren't you glad
You just cracked a smile
Aren't you glad
You're not on your last mile
Aren't you glad
Life isn't so bad
Aren't you glad

It just takes a second or maybe a minute
To gather the good and put us right in it

Aren't you glad
That we met today
Aren't you glad
We put the daggers away
Aren't you glad
That we can't stay mad
Aren't you glad

New beginnings make a new end
Aren't you glad, I know I am

Aren't you glad
That we met today
Aren't you glad
We put the daggers away
Aren't you glad
That we can't stay mad
Aren't you glad

Back at It

The Inquisition
Truth under cover
The Crusades
Fear of the other
War between the states
Brother against brother
What God really hates
Is love gone asunder

And we're right back at it
Always back at it
Don't know when to STOP
Something being tragic
Strong-willed, blood spilled
Dreams killed, hate-filled
Making our own deep shit
And we all take the hit
When we're right back at it
Always back at it

The devastation
Is blindly obscene
Firearms
Bring more gasoline
Out in the open
True lies are succeeding
Evil is climbing
And goodness retreating

And we're right back at it
Always back at it
Don't know how to STOP
Something being tragic
Strong-willed, blood spilled
Dreams killed, hate-filled
Making our own deep shit
And we all take the hit
When we're right back at it
Always back at it

If we are to be living proof
That doing good is what good does
Then help me raise the roof
So there is room for both of us

Then go right back at it
Always back at it
Knowing how to STOP
Something being tragic
Hearts filled, minds thrilled
Dreams built, hate killed
Taking care of our own shit
We'll move the needle a little bit
Then go right back at it
Always back at it

BETTER

I believed in something better, better, better
In your arms I am better better better
Every tear is disappearing
Every smile is reappearing

Long lost roads are forgotten
New-found love makes me soften
I am gifted in this moment
I am lifted in this moment
I am better I am better I am better
Better better in this moment

When I speak you always hear me hear me hear me
In my heart I keep you near me near me near me
No more shame that I once carried
Every laugh no longer buried

Long lost roads are forgotten
New-found touch makes me soften
I am changing in this moment
We're no strangers in this moment
I am better I am better I am better
Better better in this moment

No constraints around my heart
Here I am and here you are

Long lost roads are forgotten
New-found love makes me soften
I am me now more than ever
I am lifted towards forever
I am better I am better I am better
Better better in this moment

Better Self

When I don't like the world at large
And think I should be the one in charge
I check in with my foolish self
And put my ego on the lower shelf

When I hate that life is full of stress
And the best I got is a sloppy mess
Wishing I had it more together
Jealous of those who always do it better

But when I'm in love with what is real
I have little doubt about how I feel
And if I'm allowed to steal a kiss
That's a moment I don't want to miss

And when I'm in love with my better self
I play the cards that I've been dealt
And I feel the joy my heart has felt
And pass it on to someone else
When I'm in love with my better self

When I can't stand the skin I'm in
And that ugly voice takes hold again
And I spend my time covering up
The beauty I have that needs my love

When I don't have everything you've got
And feeling that way doesn't feel so hot
'Cause I'm all about the haves and have-nots
Like a long-lost soul with a blind spot

But when I'm in love with what is real
I have little doubt about how I feel
And if I believe I'm worth my dream
I won't let the darkness steal a thing

'Cause when I'm in love with my better self
I play the cards that I've been dealt
And I feel the joy my heart has felt
And pass it on to someone else
When I'm in love with my better self

Big Dreams in a Small Town

Some folks want to leave
With no reason to stay
But I wake up feeling
Just the opposite way
I like where I am
'Cause my mind's on fertile ground
I still have big dreams in a small town

I want a general store on the corner of Third and Main
Where you can get your hardware and your supply of grain
With a sign that says welcome, "Here we're all friends
Thanks for stopping by and please come back again"

And maybe I'll tell a story about how this town was born
And sweeten up some kid's day with a bag of candy corn
And in that marble jar are there more than fifty-one
The closest guess wins a trading card with a sheet of bubble gum

Some folks want to leave
With no reason to stay
But I wake up feeling
Just the opposite way
I like where I am
'Cause my heart's on fertile ground
I still have big dreams in a small town

We have no fancy theatre, just a dance hall full of cracks
You can see how grand it use to be if you peel the old paint back
And just once I want to sing there and sing "Let It Be"
And maybe bring down the house like someone did before me

Some folks want to leave
'Cause there are things we lack
But I think that simplicity
Is what always brings them back
They miss some of this
And they miss some of that
Even watching Joe DeAngelo
Parading in his Abe Lincoln hat

And then, there's that situation I have with Betty Bentley
No she doesn't own one, but we've been dating friendly
And I might be wrong, but I think she's been dropping a clue
It's time for me to plant my knee and do what lovers do

Some folks want to leave
With no reason to stay
But I wake up feeling
Just the opposite way
I like where I am
And when the sun goes down
I still have big dreams in a small town

Can't Take Back

I can't make you love yourself
I can't do it without your help
I see you closing a heart that's broken
But there must be a way to keep it open

What haven't you forgiven that keeps you from livin'
What haven't you let go of that keeps you from love

Is it something you broke that I'm sorry won't fix
Is it something you were never able to eighty-six
Is it something so blue you slip into the black
Is it something you did that you can't take back

I wonder about sadness
The good in you, you call badness
'Cause raw emotions are nature's raw deal
They're hard to explain and even harder to feel

What haven't you forgiven that keeps you from livin'
What haven't you let go of that keeps you from love

Is it something that lingers and fingers your guilt
Is it something you lost, time hasn't rebuilt
Is it something so blue you slip into the black
Is it something you did that you can't take back

I'll stand by your side, while you're working through it
When doubt often chides we'll try to undo it

Is it something you broke that I'm sorry won't fix
Is it something you were never able to eighty-six
Is it something so blue you slip into the black
Is it something you did that you can't take back

Is it something that changed you inside and out
Is it something your heart can't speak about
Is it something so blue you slip into the black
Is it something you did that you can't take back

Capture My Heart Slowly

Easy, just go easy
We don't have to rush
Let me get to know you first
Before our bodies touch

If we cross the line too soon
We're taking a big chance
'Cause love can fall away
When it happens too fast

Capture my heart slowly
It's an act of faith
Capture my heart slowly
The finest things in life
Are always worth the wait

Don't be in a hurry
Court me for a while
Show me romance isn't dead
Bring it back in style

Walk me in the moonlight
Under starry skies above
What may seem old-fashioned
Is our key to lasting love

Capture my heart slowly
It's an act of faith
Capture my heart slowly
The finest things in life
Are always worth the wait

And every day we'll build a love that will remain
'Cause we'll take the time to learn what lies beneath the flame

Capture my heart slowly
It's an act of faith
Capture my heart slowly
The finest things in life
Are always worth the wait

Church Boy

You'd think I'd be ruthless
You'd think I'd be cold
You'd think without believing
I'd be afraid for my soul

You'd think I'd be lawless
Don't know right from wrong
Screw every last one of you
Until your last dime is gone

But that's not me in any shape or form
I can feel a heart that is worn and torn
What about you, what's your excuse
That you don't walk in the Fisherman's shoes

Yeah, let's all get to the real story
Hypocrites are in their glory
Fool hardy bible quotes
Cheery picked to fool some folks
I think I have a right to know
From where all true blessings flow
But I don't search so I can destroy
I'm nothing like you, church boy

I thought love was the answer
Forgive and forget
I thought those weaker than you
Would be those you'd protect

I thought to be saved
Was a way out of hell
But you don't behave
Nearly that well

You use your faith like a lethal weapon
Where is the joy in your Sunday session
What is your game your lame excuse
That you don't walk in the Fisherman's shoes

Yeah, let's all get to the real story
Charlatans are in their glory
Happy devils making plans
Nothing moral ever stands
I think I have a right to know
From where all true blessings flow
But I don't search so I can destroy
I'm nothing like you, church boy

Yeah, let's all get to the real story
Profiteers are in their glory
Every act the bottom line
Setting traps to lead the blind
I think I have a right to know
From where all true blessings flow
But I don't search so I can destroy
Thank God I'm not a church boy

Come Home (Before It Gets Too Dark)

Go out and play
My Mama would say
But stay away from our new car
If it gets scratched
It's going to be your ass
And come home before it gets too dark

"Be here on time, 'cause dinner's at seven"
At 6:45 I heard the warning bell
I walked in with a minute to spare
Washed my hands but not very well

I was secure with my place at the table
And I didn't know how lucky I was
All the talk sounded like a busted cable
But the message was always one of love

We'll always be here
If your mind isn't clear
And the world starts weighing on your heart
The door is open
If you feel something's broken
Just come home before it gets too dark

Something to appreciate long after the fact
But I took it took heart so I could give it back

At twenty-two, he's going through a phase
It's starting to hurt that he can't find work
And a bad romance has my son in a daze
But I told him to start with the hard part first

Take a look inside
And search far and wide
And find the most resilient star
If you lose your way
And the light starts to fade
Just come home before it gets too dark

We'll always be here
If your mind isn't clear
And the world starts weighing on your heart
If you start to fall
Don't hesitate to call
Just come home before it gets too dark

Corvette

I had a Volkswagen, he had a Corvette
I wrote you love songs, he had a Corvette
In your eyes, I could do no wrong, except
I had a Volkswagen, he had a Corvette

The car that stole your heart away
What could I do, what could I say
You were revved up with a need for speed
He was all muscle and grew his own weed
Yeah, you sped off like the heat was on
Side by side with dreamboat John
What can I say that I haven't said yet
I had a Volkswagen, he had a Corvette

Well, it seems hard times hit your man of the hour
He went up in smoke with his flower power
While he rested his bones in the county jail
He sold that Corvette to help raise bail

The car that stole your heart away
Was bought by me, oh happy day
I guess karma has a way of making deals
That's me out there being hell on wheels
I can feel it up and down my spine
What once was his is now all mine
What can I say that I haven't said yet
I had a Volkswagen, he had a Corvette

I still don't have those chiseled looks
But I got a ride that really cooks

The car that stole your heart away
Is in my hands and here to stay
Yeah, I'm all revved up with a need for speed
And dreamboat John left behind some weed
I think I know what turns you on
Besides all those lines in my love songs
There's a bad boy in me you haven't met
Easy to love and hard to forget

I guess that makes me a double threat
What can I say that I haven't said yet
I had a Volkswagen, but it's all gone
He had a Corvette, but not for long

Couldn't Be Happier

Baby don't even start to shed a tear
'Cause I'm trying to shed some light
Half the time you're never here
And the other half we're only halfway right

The writing's clearly on the wall
And I volunteer to take the fall

I'm skipping out of this halfway house
'Cause some things aren't meant to be
And I couldn't be happier… for me

Baby don't even try to test my heart
'Cause I'm real testy as it is
Half of me is screaming glad
And the other half is only halfway sad

That's three quarters short of the mark
And that ain't enough to fill my heart

I'm skipping out of this halfway house
'Cause the truth will set you free
And I couldn't be happier… for me

Why stick it out through thick and thin
When there's nothing here for us to win

The writing's clearly on the wall
And I volunteer to take the fall

I'm skipping out of this halfway house
'Cause some things aren't meant to be
And I couldn't be happier… for me

CRAZY TOWN II

Will we or won't we
Ever get it together
The story never ends
It's just stormy weather

Another chapter
One for the ages
The passion burns
And the fire rages

It's a sequel with no equal
An emotional slasher
And we can't let go 'cause we love a disaster
And it's torture through and through
And I wish it weren't true, but it's
Starring none other than me and you
In Crazy Town II

Street-life has scattered
Our lips stand a-blazing
For one boy and one girl
We're no less than amazing

Our hearts empty out
High noon drawing near
We can't stand the heat
Should we break up right here?

It's a sequel with no equal
An emotional squeaker
Where after an hour love only gets weaker
And it's torture like before
But now it's even more and it's
Starring none other than me and you
In Crazy Town II

One brave citizen says this is our home
Just leave us alone and go back to parts unknown

It's a sequel with no equal
It's a kiss we can't resist
It's a real head scratcher 'cause we never find bliss
We're disfunction at the junction
And I wish it weren't true, but it's…

A sequel with no equal
An emotional teaser
And we're the bad habit in a double feature
And it's torture through and through
And I wish it weren't true, but it's
Starring none other than me and you
In Crazy Town II

Dear Aneurysm

Dear Aneurysm
At the root of my heart
I hear you're growing faster
Than your other surrounding parts

Before you burst your bubble
And create us tons of trouble
Could you give me a heads up
Maybe a clue of what to do

You have a bad reputation
For being a silent killer
But no one needs a bleeding heart
Or one that's quickly torn apart

I've been there and done that
I mean you felt it too or I hope you did
When a certain someone rejected me
That was brutal being a teenage kid

And how about many years later
When I was sure I'd found the love of my life
And when it didn't work out
You shared with me all that stress and strife

You know I didn't mean
To put you under that much pressure
But living large is what I like to do
So, how about not showing me the door
'Cause I'm sure my heart can take a little more

And, Dear Aneurysm
Please no surprise attacks
At least not one that you can't take back

Dollar Store

I got tired and impatient of being alone
I shouted to the heavens is anyone home
I guess they took offense and hurried my request
And sent me someone they thought would be best

Yes, he swept me off my feet
And then, he swept me out to sea
More alone than I was before
His shining armor from the dollar store

It was like his act was all rehearsed
And his lack of class even made it worse
So you might be thinking what was I drinking
That made me beg for such a rotten egg

Well, he found me just in time
And then, I found me without a dime
Sure enough he couldn't afford
His shining armor from the dollar store

What a con, what a jerk
Not even close to Captain Kirk

I'm going out for my morning run
I'm trying to make up for the lack of sun
I'm not wishing a thing from the gods of love
The last one came true and what a mess that was

Yes, he swept me off my feet
And then, he swept me out to sea
Lost myself on a shipwrecked shore
'Cause zero hero took a dive once more

Yes, I went and told him so
And then, I told him where to go
Had my say and guess what I wore
That shining armor from the dollar store

Got my power back and I'm ready for more
And I owe it all to the dollar store

Don't Blame Love

As much as we would like things to stay the same
Life can change and when it does
Don't blame love

Love must have its reasons
Love has many seasons
Love is there when we are falling
Love seeks a much higher calling

As much as we can see the way things should be
And when mercy doesn't come
Don't blame love

Love does not equivocate
Love advises those that hate
Love is not the deadly cancer
Love's the one and only answer

Every minute of every day
I fight the urge to not shy away from love

As much as we bend to mend a broken heart
And pain still follows us
Don't blame love

Love is there to offer help
Love can reinvent itself
Love can stand a bad decision
Love frees you from your own prison

As much as we want something better together
But we still can't rise above
Don't blame love

Love is faith put to the test
Love is peace when there's unrest
Love does not deceive itself
Love gives life to someone else

Love survives doing somersaults
Love gone wrong is no one's fault
Love is a gift from up above
Don't blame love

Don't Make Me Go There

I forget that I can walk and talk
That I can eat and sleep
That I can think for myself
And let my soul run deep

I forget that I can sing and dance
That I can laugh and cry
And if my heart tells me to
I can even say goodbye

But don't make me go there
Don't force that word from me
Don't let it touch my lips
With any kind of certainty
I think I'd rather die
Than make goodbye the thing we share
'Cause I'd go anywhere with you
But don't make me go there

I forget that I can live and learn
That I can give and take
That I can right my own ship
And leave us drowning in my wake

But don't make me go there
Don't put me in that place
Any war I win right now
In memory I'll have to face
I think I'd rather die
Than make goodbye the thing we share
'Cause I'd go anywhere with you
But don't make me go there

Unresolved issues
And boxes of tissues
And someone's at fault
Is always the end result

But don't make me go there
Don't run me out of town
Don't turn us into nothing
'Cause we'll never live it down
I think I'd rather die
Than make goodbye the thing we share
'Cause I'd go anywhere with you
But don't make me go there

EVEN IF

Even if you were filthy rich
Even if I could make you my bitch
Even if I could throw you off a cliff now and then
Even if I'll never be yours again

Even if I was horny as hell
Even if you could easily tell
Even if you were stiff Biff and you plied me with gin
Even if I'll never be yours again

Been there and did you
And you lost out buckeroo
A day late and an inch short
Sorry to give an honest report

Even if you beg on your knees
Even if you repeat pretty please
Even if you offer me that very big gem
Even if I'll never be yours again

Been there and did you
And you lost out buckeroo
Had your shot and dropped the ball
You crawling back just says it all

Even if your name wasn't Biff
Even if that would make a big diff
Even if you say Tiff you're my beginning and my end
Even if I'll never be yours again

Been there and did you
And you lost out buckeroo
A day late and an inch short
Sorry to give an honest report

Even if I could throw you off a cliff now and then
Even if I'll never be yours again

Explain Away

I can hear everything you haven't spoken
My ears are fine, though my heart is broken
But you appear to have even more to say
So please by all means explain away

Start with a drink if you think that would help
And tell me out loud there is no one else
If your mind gets cloudy, I won't interfere
I already know what's going on here

You can explain away a midnight run
You can explain away you're just having fun
You can explain away there's nothing to see
But you can't explain away what it's done to me

I can see that our world is slowly burning
My eyes are fine, though my heart is hurting
But I need to know why you want it this way
So please by all means explain away

Start with a drink if you think that would help
To come face to face with me and yourself
'Cause lie after lie won't change the fact
The truth has a way of coming back

You can explain away your dinner date
You can explain away the reason you're late
You can explain away there's nothing to see
But you can't explain away what it's done to me

Last night I looked at an empty plate
Tonight I've decided to change my fate

I'll have a drink 'cause I think that would help
And put on a face and go treat myself
And I might get lucky if not for the fact
The truth has a way of coming back

So I'll explain away my midnight run
And I'll explain away I'm just having fun
And I'll explain away there's nothing to see
But I can't explain away what it's done to me

For My Heart

We don't understand each other
And we're not one with one another
I need to go and find that spark
So, I'm leaving you for my heart

For my heart that knows me better
For my heart I can't ignore
For my heart that speaks my language
And touches me at my core
For my heart before it's broken
And I forget that love is real
For my heart that tells me letting go
Is a better way for me to feel

We're not forever, me and you
And time won't change what we can't do
Time to move on from where we are
The war is over for my heart

For my heart through cries and whispers
For my heart that needs to breathe
For my heart that knows I can't hold you
'Cause the weight is too much for me
For my heart before it's broken
And I forget that love is real
For my heart that tells me letting go
Is a better way for me to feel

For my heart that gives me shelter
Through the thick and thin of pain
For my heart that knows between us
We have nothing left to gain
For my heart before it's broken
And I forget that love is real
For my heart that tells me letting go
Is a better way for me to feel

For my heart and for yours too
And for all that we've been through
For my heart and for the next step
And for love without regret

Friends Only

One day it wasn't and the next day it was
Just like that as a matter of fact
One day it wasn't and the next day it was, love

Through and through, me and you
And we said shit, now what do we do
You told me once you'd never get that lonely
And I swore we were born to be friends only

Now look at us
We crossed the line
From never before
To there's always a first time
I mean who knew, I didn't, did you
Stars in the eyes took us by surprise
Little did we know we'd let that side of us show
One day it wasn't and the next day it was, love

That night together and the next night too
Something real that changed how we feel
A whole new level and the real us was, love

Through and through, me and you
And we said shit, now what do we do
You told me once you'd never get that lonely
And I swore we were born to be friends only

Now look at us
Smiling away
'Cause friends only
Faded away yesterday
I mean who knew, I didn't, did you
Stars in the eyes we couldn't disguise
Little did we know like Juliet and Romeo
One day it wasn't and the next day it was, love

Something you think is going to be ruined
Until you find out it was worth pursuin'

Must be that chemistry and a similar need
Do you think two drinks made us do the deed
One day it wasn't and the next day it was, love

Now look at us
We're doing fine
And I am yours
And you are mine for all time
I know it's true and you know it too
'Cause love never dies with a friend by your side
And that's how we know we'll never let go

One day it wasn't and the next day it was
Just like that as a matter of fact
One day it wasn't and the next day it was, love

Full Dream Ahead

I'm into you and you're into me
Sometimes what's good is to let it be
Let it take its course, let it ride the rails
No tearful regrets if this moment fails

The day is ours
The night is too
I'm thinking tomorrow
I'll wake up with you

Full dream ahead
The stars at our back
We can come up for air
Somewhere down the track
Let the chance take hold
Let our love be bold
Yeah, enough said
Full dream ahead

It's no wonder I feel spellbound and
Maybe baby we found wonderland
I know one thing, you're really some thing
Call me a fool, I don't care to be cool

The day is ours
The night is too
I'm thinking tomorrow
It's all me and you

Full dream ahead
Stack up the cards
Let them fall where they may
Let us be who we are
Let the lovebird sing
We can do anything
Yeah, enough said
Full dream ahead

It's as true as it seems
So, I'm sticking with you
As we're picking up steam

Full dream ahead
And the time is now
You got one heart to steal
And I'll show you how
Let the chance take hold
Let our love be bold
Yeah, enough said
Full dream ahead

Fun Fact

We did that once
At the drop of a hat
Kinda hard now
To get that magic back
But here we meet again
Right out of the blue
And something's going on
That's always been true

Fun fact: opposites attract
Sometimes it's a deal
And you find your perfect match
Sometimes it gets rocky
And you want to roll it back
But sometimes it's just a fun fact
Opposites attract

You were too tall
Talked a mile a minute
I was so sure
My heart wasn't in it
But an hour went by
And then two and then ten
In a matter of time
It was your place or mine

Fun fact: opposites attract
Sometimes it's a meal
And sometimes it's a snack
Sometimes it's make-believe
And it's only good for that
But sometimes it's just a fun fact
Opposites attract

It must be this familiar place
'Cause all I want to do is kiss your face

Fun fact: opposites attract
Sometimes it's a feel
And it really is all that
And sometimes it's an itch
You just really have to scratch
But sometimes it's just a fun fact
Opposites attract

Yeah, sometimes you get lucky
And you find your perfect match
But sometimes it's just a fun fact
Opposites attract

Get It While It's Hot

I may not look this good forever
And I'm so uncool when we're together
But I got some sizzle in just the right spot
So get it while it's hot

I may not walk with smoking swagger
But I'm trying to do my best Mick Jagger
And you're welcome baby, 'cause it takes a lot
So get it while it's hot

Don't just sit there and soak in the sights
I got the fire started so do me right
Like the pavement burning under your feet
I have no intention to turn down the heat

I may not beguile after awhile
But I can cook something up only wearing a smile
And I taste a lot better than a tater-tot
So get it while it's hot

Don't just sit there and soak in the sights
I got the fire started so hold me tight
Like the sunshine baking a sandy beach
I have no intention to turn down the heat

Baby, life is short but my legs are long
And it's all out there 'cause I'm wearing a thong

Don't just sit there and soak in the sights
I got the fire started so do me right
Like the warm sensation under the sheets
I have no intention to turn down the heat

Baby, I'm your flame, I brighten your day
And you let me shine and I like it that way

I may not look this good forever
And I'm so uncool when we're together
But I got some sizzle in just the right spot
So get it while it's hot

Getting Started

I'm going to wrap this misery in shiny paper
Send it down the river sooner than later
Include a goodbye with a tearful letter
And leave fearful behind so I can get better

I'll stop looking for love and look after myself
Now that's a sweet deal like nothing else
And make no excuse for what use to be true
I gave up myself when I gave in to you

Though I'm slightly blinded
I'm still strong-minded
Though I feel mistreated
I'm far from defeated

Got a new dream brewing won't sit around stewing
Whatever I've done won't be my undoing
Yeah, you've gone your way and I'm going mine
But I know in my soul it'll work out fine

I'll put on that dress and let it snuggle me tight
Better it than you 'cause you wronged me right
I'll wear it loose on my shoulders and set it loose on the world
'Cause I'm making it known that I'm my own girl

Though my course is altered
My heart hasn't faltered
And the night has departed
And the day's getting started

When I have those moments that drive me insane
I'll call Sweet Laughter to reduce my pain
And when I lose sleep that I need so badly
Then I'll just dig deep and do it gladly

I'm going to wrap this misery in shiny paper
Send it down the river sooner than later
Include a goodbye with a tearful letter
And leave fearful behind so I can get better

Though I'm slightly blinded
I'm still strong-minded
And the night has departed
And the day's getting started

Halftime

Are you ready Freddy for sexy Betsy
She's bringing her friend her sexy bestie
They want to meet us under the bleachers
In that secret place away from the teachers

When halftime comes and the band starts to play
That's our cue to start sneaking away
And don't make a stop at the hot dog stand
Eating one or two could spoil our plan

'Cause you won't get a kiss with ketchup breath
And don't show for a second you're scared to death
If you're nervous at all, you got to hide it man
They don't want a boy with a sweaty hand

Are you ready Freddy for sexy Betsy
And Destiny her sexy bestie
I hear she likes to stare in your eyes
So don't act the fool, just bring on the cool

'Cause twenty minutes is the halftime limit
So make it worth every minute you're in it
If you're sucking face, don't get all profound
It's going to be hit and run with people around

And we don't want the girls to think we don't care
So say some nice things but don't overshare
After all, Monday they'll be walking down the hall
And you want that note that says give me a call

Now, we've been friends from the very first grade
And this is your first shot at the big parade
So, one piece of advice and I hope this will help
You can grab her hand but don't grab anything else

If all goes well there will be time for that
So, don't mess this up is what I'm driving at
'Cause I know Betsy and her very hot bestie
Are the right girls to change our world

And I got your back and you got mine
'Cause we got a whole lot on the line
At halftime

HAPPY HEART

Yes, it hurts when love doesn't last
But I have no wish to review the past
It may be sad that we grew apart
But I go to bed with a happy heart

You're not just a memory tucked away
You're the reason I am where I am today
And I hope for you, I've played the same part
And you go to bed with a happy heart

Happy for you and happy for me
That we left each other for calmer seas
Knowing better together only went so far
We were smart to depart with a happy heart

Our lives have taken many good turns
And the light you brought me forever burns
'Cause we made goodbye a walk in the park
And we made our peace with a happy heart

Happy for you and happier too
That someone found me and someone found you
Knowing we were no match in each other's arms
We were smart to depart with a happy heart

Our moment came and our moment went
But there's nothing with you I'll ever lament

Happy for us and happier still
We were willing to see what we couldn't fulfill
Knowing better together wasn't in the stars
We were smart to depart with a happy heart

Happy for you and happy am I
That we see each other with loving eyes
Knowing nothing is better than where we are
We were smart to depart with a happy heart

HE WATCHES ME

It's not Halloween, but it's a Halloween night!
The moonlight breaking through my bedroom blinds
has cast the face of a demonic creature on my wall.
He watches me. He hovers over me like a bad nightmare.

I hide under the covers and occasionally, bravely, I peek out
to see if his appetite for scaring seven-year-olds is completely
satiated. A quick glance with the thought of "please don't eat me"
crosses my mind. As I cross my fingers, I hope to last at least a
minute or two more in my young life.

I can't call out for help that would only make this monster angrier.
I begin to sweat. I start to fret. I don't know what that word means yet,
but boy oh boy am I upset. I tell myself you've got to be brave,
now is not the time to cave.

Finally, breaking through this horrible terror, it occurs to me
if I pull the cord on the window blinds, I will destroy this ugly intruder
and I will banish him forever from my room.

His time is up and my time has come, I say, as I gather my courage, take the chance, explode from the safety of my comforter and defiantly reach for the cord. Yes! I've got it and with a once in a lifetime yank, I close the blinds and slowly, ever so carefully look back.

I've done it. He has disappeared, no doubt running scared from my will to defeat him. My will that only grew stronger and stronger. And now he watches me no longer!

Heard That Story Before

I've heard that story before
So before you tell it again
Could you change the part where I broke your heart
And your sanity got razor thin

'Cause I've heard about how I was trouble
I've heard about the way things went
I've heard about who was to blame
And how your precious tears were spent
I've heard about our rise and fall
Over and over I've heard it all
Even that part where you call me a whore
Yeah, I've heard that story before

I've entertained your reasons
I've listened while I flinched with pain
Could you change the part who you think you are
Is a victim with a slandered name

'Cause I've heard about all your goodness
And how I treated you so bad
I've heard about your love for me
And you were the best I ever had
I've heard a number of your lies
Under the cover of you really tried
But that tall tale doesn't sail anymore
'Cause I've heard that story before

You can't excuse your misdemeanors
It doesn't make you come out cleaner
You scorched the earth under our feet
That's the reality I'd like you to meet

'Cause I've heard about my deception
I've heard about your perfect self
I've heard when we were together
You never looked at anyone else
I've heard about your brand-new love
That she's everything I never was
Until she walked right out that door
And left you where you've been before

I've heard a number of your lies
Under the cover of you really tried
But that's a con and nothing more
'Cause I've heard that story before

I Believe in Us

I don't believe in the hands of fate
I don't believe in star dust
I don't believe in some moonlit meant to be
But I believe in us

The way we zig and zag together
The way a snag only makes us better
The way I feel self-assured
When I rest my heart at night with yours
The way we sing our own sweet song
The way we go merrily along
Even when there's a cloud of dust
I believe in us

I don't believe we met with prayer
I don't believe in cupid much
I don't believe in some pre-made destiny
But I believe in us

The way we march our hearts together
The way you make my day much better
The way you feel in my arms
When I let myself let down my guard
The way we earn each other's trust
The way we learn to trust in love
Even those times we self-destruct
I believe in us

The way we take and the way we give
The way each day we choose to live
The way we rise and the way we fall
And the way we don't back off at all

The way we zig and zag together
The way a snag only makes us better
The way I feel self-assured
When I rest my heart at night with yours
The way we sing our own sweet song
The way we go merrily along
Even when there's a cloud of dust
I believe in us

I Could've Handled Things Better

I just want to say I reacted with shock
I've let it all go, but I do have thoughts
When I found out you cheated I reached down deep
And I came up with this in my sleep

I could've handled things better
I could've shot you dead
I could've unloaded on you
Until I ran out of lead
I could've jumped for joy
You were forever gone
And buried you ass
On your girlfriend's lawn
I could've laughed out loud
That you deserved what you got
I could've handled things better
Whether better or not

I'm a gentle soul and a harmless fly
But not when you leave tears in my eyes
You got your way of dealing and I got mine
But I left this out when you crossed the line

I could've handled things better
Put your body on display
Showed all of your friends
Things don't always go your way
I could've thanked my stars
You belong where you are
Like the OK Corral
Resting next to a pal
I could've walked on your grave
And it would've made my day
I could've handled things better
In a much better way

I'm sorry that I underreacted
I handed my forgiveness to you
I'd like to make up for that
And tell you what I meant to do

I could've handled things better
I couldn't said to God
I'm gonna do me some damage
With a cattle prod
I could've crossed my heart
And hoped you'd die
And buried your ass
One piece at a time
I could've laughed out loud
That you deserved what you got
I could've handled things better
Whether better or not

I Don't Know How

All my love for him has gone away
I can't be here another day
My only dream is getting out
The problem is I don't know how

He's always right, I'm always wrong
I'm called a bitch all day long
He's getting worse with his abuse
It's because of me that's his excuse

With an ounce of courage in my heart
I make a run, but don't get far
My only dream is getting out
The problem is I don't know how

I try to appease, I try to please
I call my friends, I call the police
They believe him, but never me
So, I just get more of his disease

He wants to know everywhere I go
He wants me to call every hour or so
He's out of control and doesn't care
I want to leave but I really don't dare

I can't just walk, he'll hunt me down
And I can't survive with him around
With vile words only evil would say
He threatens to take my child away

I try to cajole, I try to persuade
I try to not show I'm deeply afraid
But he believes he owns all of me
So, I just get more of his disease

I need someone before it's too late
To help me find a way to escape
My only dream is getting out
The problem is I don't know how

I Found the Secret

I found the secret to my mind
It likes to be explored
I found the secret to my body
It likes to be adored

I found the secret and I won't give it up
From one to ten it's a ten and above
It's nothing less than a dream come true
I found the secret and the secret is you

I found the secret to a kiss
It strikes the perfect chord
I found the secret to desire
It hates to be ignored

I found the secret and it's mine all mine
From one to ten it's a ninety-nine
It's nothing less than a dream come true
I found the secret and the secret is you

Beyond any words beyond any doubt
You know I can't keep it, the secret is out

I found the secret to my heart
It loves an open book
I found the secret to my soul
So, come and take a look

I found the secret and I won't give it up
From one to ten it's a ten and above
It's nothing less than a dream come true
I found the secret and the secret is you

I found the secret and it's mine all mine
From one to ten it's a ninety-nine
It's nothing less than a dream come true
I found the secret and the secret is you

I Want to Be Happy

I was told that to be my very best self
I had to truly love me like no one else
Kick all those demons to the roadside curb
And drink only tea with organic herbs

And so, I did, and never looked back
I'm clean as a whistle and sharp as a tack
I can't tell you how healthy I feel
But I'm just not me and that's a big deal

I want to have curves
I want to be happy
Give me sinfully sweet
And make it snappy
I want to eat something
That is bad for me
I want to be happy
Like I used to be

What does it matter if I lose a few pounds
If I lose my smile and there's no one around
I think I'll get back to my more beautiful self
That person who can't always tighten their belt

I want to have curves
I want to be happy
No peas or carrots
'Cause they taste crappy
I want to have my cake
And eat it guilt free
I want to be happy
Like I used to be

I'm not going to obsess about staying thin
If I don't feel good about the body I'm in

I want to have curves
I want to be happy
Give me that pizza
And make it snappy
I want to round things out
And do it guilt free
I want to be happy
Like I used to be

I know, I know, I've got to watch my weight
Maybe tomorrow, 'cause tonight it's too late

I want to have curves
I want to be happy
Give me sinfully sweet
And make it snappy
I want to round things out
And do it guilt free
I want to be happy
So, be happy for me

I'm Going With You

That voice of the past
Doesn't have long to last
The future has bigger plans
Though the dream is bolder
I'm right on your shoulder
No matter the shifting sands

Wherever you want to go
I'm going with you
If you'll have me, let's begin
My heart is all in
I'm ready to travel on dirt or gravel
Or walk the smoothest avenue
Take me near or far, but as far as you go
I'm going with you

The adventure starts
On the promise of hearts
That knows the song of the sparrow
When life turns on a dime
There's no question it's time
To widen the straight and narrow

Wherever you want to go
I'm going with you
If you'll have me, let's begin
My heart is all in
I'm ready to travel on dirt or gravel
Unravel a mystery or two
Either fast or slow, but as long as you go
I'm going with you

Whatever you're seeking in your heart and mind
I want to be a part of whatever you find

Wherever you want to go
I'm going with you
If you'll have me, let's begin
My heart is all in
I'm ready to travel on dirt or gravel
To where that field of dreams comes true
Take me high or low, but as far as you go
I'm going with you

In That Line

If I could read it out loud to you
I think you'd hear it the way I do
Certain words need an emphasis
And there's not one I want you to miss

In that line that says I'm sorry
Sorry is what I mean
'Cause I'm thinking of us at home
Without you feeling so alone

And in that line that says forgive me
I mean I'll do better
To always keep your hand in mine
And that's not just another line

If there's something we're not done with
And you believe we are more than this
Let me try to convince you why
We could talk it out without goodbye

In that line that says together
I mean I get it now
Better to run into your arms
Than even think of running out

And in that line that says I'm learning
I hope you see that's true
In me I have some gold to mine
And that's not just another line

I want these words to find new meaning
So we might find a way to healing

In that line that says I'm breaking
I mean shaking my past
And I'm praying there's still a chance
Your heart might slowly take me back

And in that line that says forever
I mean I'll do better
And I know we'll get there in time
And that's not just another line

I know we'll get there in time
And that's not just another line

INTUITIVE

At the end of the day
There's a place in my heart
You occupy
It never goes away
No matter where you are
And I know why

It just breathes
It just lives
It's love that's intuitive
It just knows
It just is
It's love that's intuitive

As the night gently calls
There's a place in the stars
I can't deny
It never loses light
And it shines near and far
And I know why

It just breathes
It just lives
It's love that's intuitive
It just knows
It just is
It's love that's intuitive

Since the moment of birth
There is a soul to unearth

It just breathes
It just lives
It's love that's intuitive
It just knows
It just is
It's love that's intuitive

Is This a Bad Time

You didn't expect me but here I am
And you and your playmate are hogging our bed
So, just one question you low-life swine
Is this a bad time?

I could turn back the clock
Free my hand from this rock
Maybe move down the block
If that's what you need
Even join in the fun
Do a real one and done
Maybe blow your mind some
But believe me that will never be our reality

I must say I stand here all amazed
The dog is barking and we are both crazed
So, just one question before I lose my mind
Is this a bad time?

I could cover my eyes
You could cover your lies
We could wear that cheap disguise
If that's what you need
Even contemplate
How close love is to hate
And bend but never break
But believe me that will only be in your dreams

You have seconds before I'm locked and loaded
You should write that down so in court it's noted
You can use it later on the show Dateline
You no-good swine

Yeah, before you get up and fly down the stairs
You shouldn't confuse me with someone who shares
Unless of course it's your very last dime
'Cause that's the first thing I'm claiming as mine

I should just clean your clock
Mister dumb as a rock
With a head like a block
'Cause you forgot to think
You took off your ring
To diddle your thing
But it's going to sting
'Cause believe me you're about to see Queen Bee

What's the matter, have you lost your tongue?
There's someone here who could give you some
So before I send you where the sun don't shine
Nothing like the present to confess your crime
Or is this a bad time?

It Could Be

It could be
Right out of the blue
Completely unexpected
But undeniably true

It could be
A thoughtful thunderbolt
That awakens my mind
And gives my spirit a jolt

It could be
As simple as you with me
Finding the love between us
And setting it free
So, it could be

It could be
The bells are chiming
Completely accidental
But perfect timing

It could be
A thunderous roar
That awakens my heart
And lets my spirit just soar

It could be
As simple as you with me
Finding the love between us
And setting it free
So, it could be

I'm sure there is a secret code
That we could set to loving mode

It could be
The fates aligning
Or the stars above
Are redesigning

It could be
As simple as you with me
Finding the love between us
And setting it free
So, it could be

It Was a Good Day

I woke up this morning all in one piece
First cup of coffee put me right at ease
And my mind had nothing bad to say
It was a good day

I went humming to work and I came singing home
That C major seven has a really high note
I couldn't reach it but I tried anyway
It was a good day

I count myself lucky
As lucky as one could be
I got rhyme with rhythm
On what matters to me

A friend to the end called to just check in
I said, I climbed all those steps up that hill again
And my bad knee wasn't even in play
It was a good day

I cleaned out the clutter behind the closet door
I had more memories than I had room for
But that picture of us I'll never throw away
It was a good day

I count myself gifted
'Cause the gifts keep coming
I can tell in my heart
What's real and what's loving

I unplugged a thought that was burning me out
I dug something up that was keeping me down
I turned something bad into something okay
It was a good day

I crawled into bed with my body at rest
I told myself dream on, please be my guest
And my mind had nothing bad to say
And I went to sleep feeling okay
It was a good day

It's Hard to Hate Up Close

You tell lies about each other
You've given up on what is true
You intend to do them damage
Like the damage done to you

What do you think will happen
When the rubber meets the road
It's easy to go down mean street
But it's hard to hate up close

I'm sure you like the distance
You're in your comfort zone
You can gather all your forces
So you don't feel alone
You can harbor all your feelings
And carry them like a cross
You can name the name of who's to blame
For all that you have lost

You've only seen your enemy
In the papers or on TV
You've been convinced ever since
If they were gone, you'd be free

What do you think will happen
When a bad seed is sown
It's easy to chant and rave and rant
But it's hard to hate up close

I'm sure you won't buckle
You'll keep your steely pride
You'll stand firm, you won't squirm
Or run away and hide
But you might be taken by surprise
When you go eye to eye
That across from you is someone who
Might suffer just as much as you

You've never met this nemesis
But you fear them anyway
You can feel their constant threat
In what they do and what they say

What do you think will happen
When the spinning wheel gets real
And you finally land blow after blow
To show the depth of how you feel

What do you think will happen
If you find out you are wrong
And this villain that torments you
Was just a person all along

What do you think will happen
When the rubber meets the road
It's easy to go down mean street
But it's hard to hate up close

Karen's Song

You've been a friend as long as I can remember
Through thick and thin and the coldest Decembers
A park bench in the city was our first meeting place
You were always much more than your beautiful face

We weren't meant for each other but we were meant to last
When we talk on the phone it's like no time has passed
We open new worlds that we want to explore
And revive old stories we need to tell once more

Heartache and work and husbands and wives
We've been at the source through the course of our lives
And you've been a rock to everyone you touch
And I am one soul who can't thank you enough
You've embraced my life whether right or wrong
So, I give you this kiss called Karen's song

There's a picture I have on my grand piano
You were tall and I was all of five feet something small
But I felt larger than life in your presence that night
It was like Asbury Park took my heart outright

Children and work and husbands and wives
You've been at the source through the course of our lives
Yes, you've been a rock to everyone you touch
That's just one reason why I love you so much
You've cherished my dreams and encouraged me on
So, I give you this kiss called Karen's song

So many times you come last on your list
That's just who you are that's just how it is

Heartache and work and husbands and wives
You've been at the source through the course of our lives
Yes, you've been a rock to everyone you touch
And I am one soul who can't thank you enough

The thread that we share will never be gone
Always palm to palm is where we belong
So, I give you this kiss called Karen's song

KATIE JUNE

I'm getting new wheels soon
And I'm leaving this town
Will you leave with me too
Katie June

There's more for us to see out there
I can't stay here without a prayer
I've used them all and none will do
And no one understands but you

I can't do this alone
You are my heart and home
And that's always been true
Katie June

They're promises I want to make
And feelings that I just can't fake
Right now the world is just us two
'Cause I don't see me without you

I've wanted this since I was twelve
That was my wish at the wishing well

I'm holding on to hope
This time we really go
And make a dream come true
Katie June

I'm getting my ride ready
And I'm leaving this town
Will you ride with me too
Until we can't be found

I'm in love with you
Katie June

I'm in love with you
Katie June

Light on Love Heavy on Shame

Convince you, you're bad again and again
Your sins are so many they never end
In the eyes of God you're nothing but slime
Repent, repent before you run out of time

Go anywhere to a nearby church
It feels like the devil got there first
The Prince of Peace has left you alone
Your being eaten alive in the judgement zone

Light on love and heavy on shame
Fear is always the name of the game
A bunch of crap dropped in your lap
To reel you in and bring you back
Reminding you that you have a boss
That died for you up on that cross
The Christian way to fan the flames
Light on love and heavy on shame

And don't even blink and don't make a stink
You're here to obey, you're not here to think
So, be a good girl and be a good boy
'Cause life is not yours to fully enjoy

Go anywhere to a nearby church
It feels like the devil got there first
The Prince of Peace has left you alone
Your being eaten alive in the judgement zone

Light on love and heavy on shame
Fear is always the name of the game
Whoever you thought you were before
Was just a poor spirit and nothing more
Reminding you you'll suffer His wrath
If you dare to walk your own path
Control the soul is a wicked game
Light on love and heavy on shame

The message is clear and the message is sick
An hour of power with the same old schtick

Light on love and heavy on shame
Fear is always the name of the game
Guilty as charged the day before
But redemption is yours saith the Lord
Reminding you that you have a boss
That died for you up on that cross
The Christian way to fan the flames
Light on love and heavy on shame

The Christian way to fan the flames
Light on love and heavy on shame

LONELY

Men only
Women only
Whites only
Blacks only
It's all baloney, it's all phony
It's no wonder we're all so very lonely

It's going to take some bigger hearts
To fit us into Noah's Ark
It's going to take a wider bridge
For us to see where heaven is

God only
Fate only
Straight only
Gay only
It's all baloney, it's all phony
It's no wonder we're all so very lonely

It's going to take a brighter sun
To shine a light on everyone
It's going to take a stronger wind
To deliver us the mighty Quinn

Society's anxiety
Separateness and feeling less

Rich only
Famous only
Me only
You only
It's all baloney, it's all phony
It's no wonder we're all so very lonely

It's going to take a poet's spell
To tell us of a deeper well
It's going to take some lessons learned
To underscore and overturn

Men only
Women only
Me only
You only
It's all baloney, it's all phony
It's no wonder we're all so very lonely

Love Gets Better

I'm dating your ex and you're dating mine
What you didn't see in him I'm seeing just fine
So thanks for tossing him my way
And when we're crossing paths someday
I just want to say no offense intended
But whatever you broke in that man's heart
Is now completely mended

Everyone needs some healing
I'm sure you can share that feeling
And no one is a perfect fit
But all it took was a love like this
To see his smile a mile wide
Light back up with a sense of pride
Someone's trash is someone's treasure
When you find the right home love gets better

It was him and you, now it's him and me
He's everything you said he'd never be
And I'm so glad we made the swap
But this is where the trading stops
Your deal breakers are my deal makers
And whatever he thought he was doing wrong
He can keep on doing, all night long

Everyone needs some healing
I'm sure you can share that feeling
Not everyone belongs together
And sometimes love is not forever
But someone's loss is someone's gain
And I have no pleasure if you're in pain
But your ex for me is my sweetest treasure
When you find the right home love gets better

And this may sound like a bunch of jargon
But I do think I got the best of this bargain

Everyone needs some healing
I'm sure you can share that feeling
And no one is a perfect fit
But let's get down to the nitty grit
I hope for you there is no next
And life begins and ends with my ex
And you'll play house forever together
When you find the right home love gets better

Everyone needs some healing
I'm sure you can share that feeling
And no one is a perfect fit
But I got the one who's close to it
To see his smile a mile wide
Light back up with star-crossed eyes
Someone's trash is someone's treasure
And our happiness is beyond measure
When you find the right home love gets better

Mia

Did you know that Mia means a shrine or palace
A glorious place you want to be
Did you know that Mia is an ageless beauty
And finds beauty in her friends like me

Did you know that Mia has a searching soul
And in her journey, I find her brave
Did you know that Mia learns from memories
That she's not afraid to save

Her inner life is strong and true
Though she would probably say not so
It's easy to recognize dignity
'Cause she carries it wherever she goes

Did you know that Mia is a lover of art
A devotee to the muse of the heart
Did you know that Mia is at ease in her skin
Playing the bass guitar or the violin

Did you know that Mia keeps dreaming a dream
That she knows she hasn't yet sung
Did you know that Mia will never stop trying
No matter how old or how young

She reaches out for something more
That can match the passion she feels
To set in motion a healing fire
That's been quietly underseal

Did you know that Mia really loves her name
And I love that she loves it too
Did you know that Mia owns all of herself
In what she does or doesn't do

Her inner life is strong and fierce
Though she would probably say not so
It's easy to recognize dignity
'Cause she carries it wherever she goes

Did you know that Mia means a shrine or palace
A glorious place you want to be
Did you know that Mia is an ageless beauty
And finds beauty in her friends like me

Midnight Med

I took a midnight med
So I could go to sleep
I bought some midday magic
To put more pep in my step

I stopped for a drink
On my way home from work
Just to take the edge off
I thought two wouldn't hurt

I fixed a little dinner
And had a nightcap at home
Just me and some bad TV
'Cause I hate to eat alone

I had a splitting headache
So I took something for the pain
It only made me jumpy
And did a number on my brain

Somewhere close to twelve a.m.
I finally collapsed into bed
I started to weep, but I needed my sleep
So I took a midnight med

More Than Qualified (to Be My Lover)

If you show up late or maybe not at all
Forget my number so you can skip the call
And tell me I'm not as cute as my brother
Then you're more than qualified to be my lover

If you've been married at least three times
And use someone for their nickels and dimes
And will no doubt cheat and run for cover
Then you're more than qualified to be my lover

'Cause I know how to pick 'em
I have that magic touch
I know that cupid hates me
And he shows me just how much
If there's a law of attraction
I attract the very worst
'Cause I know how to pick 'em
If I can get to 'em first

If you're the opposite of what I need
And like to see a lonely heart bleed
And the lies you tell are as smooth as butter
Then you're more than qualified to be my lover

If you tell me I'm not your type at all
And you drink as much as Niagara Falls
And you like to leave town like the road runner
Then you're more than qualified to be my lover

'Cause I know how to pick 'em
I have that magic touch
I know that cupid hates me
And he shows me just how much
If there's a law of attraction
I attract the very worst
'Cause I know how to pick 'em
From the last one to the first

I've told myself to be a lot more picky
But I went back to the well for icky Vicky

If you look at me and you're on the take
'Cause I got a habit I just can't break
And you can't stay long enough for a short supper
Then you're more than qualified to be my lover

'Cause I know how to pick 'em
I have that magic touch
I know that cupid hates me
And he shows me just how much
If there's a law of attraction
I attract the very worst
'Cause I know how to pick 'em
If I can get to 'em first

My Heart Wins the Day

Two voices I hear and the devil's at play
Opposite thoughts with too much to say
When my mind is at war and I'm losing my way
When the battle is on my heart wins the day

My trusted advisor
My doctor on call
My true decider
And my know it all
My endless defender
My warrior king
The master of me
If I am listening

Two choices I have and they both feel strong
Is one more right and the other less wrong?
When I have to commit 'cause life's better that way
When the battle is on my heart wins the day

My noble protector
My window of light
My bullshit detector
When I'm losing the fight
My holy of holies
My warrior king
The master of me
If I am listening

The reasons are many for what any of us do
But when the bell tolls for me my heart rings true

My trusted advisor
My doctor on call
My true decider
And my know it all
My captain o' captain
At the river's end
My timely companion
When I need a friend

My holy of holies
My warrior king
The master of me
If I am listening

My Heroes Weren't Perfect

Disney died from cigarette smoke
Elvis and drugs wasn't a joke
Hank drank himself to an early grave
And Martin wasn't as faithful as he was brave

My heroes weren't perfect
And I forget that sometimes
My heroes weren't perfect
But they were heroes of mine

They made me laugh, they made me cry
They made me rise, they made me fall
They made me see the humanity in me
And they were flawed, but then aren't we all

Janis had a friend in heroin
Van Gogh couldn't find peace in his mind
Juliet was impulsive but strong
And Romeo's fate was love gone wrong

My heroes weren't perfect
And I forget that sometimes
My heroes weren't perfect
But they were heroes of mine

They made me care, they made me feel
They made me dream beyond what's real
They made me see the humanity in me
And they were flawed, but then aren't we all

Amy died out of sheer neglect
Washington lied at least once I bet
Robert the Bruce was the outlaw king
Billy the Kid kind of did the same thing

My heroes weren't perfect
And I forget that sometimes
My heroes weren't perfect
But they were heroes of mine

They were mythical, they were desperadoes
They were all of us, sometimes notorious
They made me see the humanity in me
And they were flawed, but then aren't we all

My Way of Drinking

I got my own style as you can see
You can judge for yourself and get back to me
You may not be thinking what I'm thinking
But I hope you come around to my way of drinking

A glass of flirtation
With two shots of together
Three bottles of kisses
And a case of forever
Four rounds of I'm happy
With five mixers of love
Six Forget Me Nots
And seven dreams to chug

I think you'll see as the night goes on
That you and I just might get along
You may not be thinking what I'm thinking
But I hope you come around to my way of drinking

A glass of vibration
With two shots of believin'
Three bottles of wishes
And a case of not leavin'
Four rounds of I'm buzzing
With five chasers of love
Six Forget Me Nots
And seven dreams to chug

You know love on the rocks can mean something sour
But in my way of drinking, it's a sweet happy hour

A glass of temptation
With two shots of tender
Three bottles of kisses
And a case of surrender
Four rounds of we're smiling
With five swigs of love
Six Forget Me Nots
And seven dreams to chug

Four rounds of we're buzzing
With High Fives of love
Six Forget Me Nots
And seven dreams straight up

Not Today, Not Tomorrow, Not Ever

I know promises can be hard to keep
But my feelings are more than just skin deep
'Cause you and I should never come cheap

I won't sell you a line that you'd never buy
I won't kick up a storm for no reason why
I won't drive us apart on this road together
Not today, not tomorrow, not ever

I won't offer the stars unless I have one to give
I won't let time slip away as long as I live
I won't fall for the myth that greener is better
Not today, not tomorrow, not ever

I know promises are easily broken
But some deserve a chance to be spoken
'Cause we always said we'd be that open

I won't follow my heart unless it leads me to you
I won't see this dream only halfway through
I won't load up the truck unless we're in it together
Not today, not tomorrow, not ever

I won't work every day, but not work at this
I won't stare at your lips without wanting a kiss
I won't forget goodnight as we drift off together
Not today, not tomorrow, not ever

I know promises can be hard to keep
But my feelings are more than just skin deep
'Cause you and I should never come cheap
Not today, not tomorrow, not ever

On the Hook

I met a woman, we met for drinks
She brought her charm, I brought my smile
We spent the night, it went so right
We brought each other into denial

We aimed to please, we aimed to tease
We caught the old love-bug disease
But we made it worth each other's while
Put all our chips in one big pile

Unrestricted, quickly addicted
Heart break coming self-inflicted

Maybe getting there is half the fun
But the other half is never done
From the fire into the frying pan
I can tell you now that wasn't the plan
From sizzling hot to we better not
We did anyway and did it a lot
The road less taken ain't the one we took
That's what happens when you're on the hook

I have to admit, after we split
We left a trail too big to fail
I looked her up, she looked me down
The moment was rigged so we set sail

Unrestricted, quickly addicted
Head winds coming as predicted

Maybe getting there is half the fun
But the other half is never done
From the fire into the frying pan
I can tell you now that wasn't the plan
From sizzling hot to we better not
We did anyway and got what we got
A lot of playtime without a playbook
That's what happens when you're on the hook

We aimed to please, we aimed to tease
We caught the old skin-deep disease
You get the gist of moonlit trysts
The night makes light of what persists

Unrestricted, quickly addicted
Heart break coming self-inflicted

Maybe getting there is half the fun
But the other half is never done
From the fire into the frying pan
I can tell you now that wasn't the plan
From sizzling hot to we better not
We did anyway and did it a lot
We loved the cover but hated the book
That's what happens when you're on the hook

From sizzling hot to we better not
We did anyway and did it a lot
The road less taken ain't the one we took
That's what happens when you're on the hook

One More Thing to Worry About

My bank account is growing thin
And I've acquired a double chin
My truck doesn't run and I'm out of beer
And our love is dead but you're still here

And now you tell me without a doubt
You'll still come around after you move out
And to that I say, well isn't that great
One more thing to worry about

The politicians are out of touch
Prices are rising way too much
My favorite team is a cellar dweller
And my singing voice is less than stellar

And now you tell me you made a vow
To be my true Boo forever somehow
And to that I say, well isn't that great
One more thing to worry about

They say leave your worries at the door
But somehow life just brings you more

Had no clothes on in my latest dream
Naked on the cover of field and stream
Found my dog at the lost and found
Lost him again to a basset hound

And now you tell me you have no doubt
That fate 'ill step in and turn us around
And to that I say, well isn't that great
One more thing to worry about

Yeah, I guess for me there's no way out
You'll be my angel if heaven allows
And to that I say, well isn't that great
One more thing to worry about

Other Side of Last Year

Last year was rough
Had to be tougher than tough
My skin was coming undone
My only one had up and run

Fell to my knees
And always asking why me
That's as honest as I can be
But coming apart set something free
It made me see the depth of me

I'm on the other side of last year
In a different headspace
In a "been there, now I'm here" place
Might even cry and look to the sky
Feeling the weight of a healing tear
But I'm on the other side of last year

Up off the floor
Eyes open knowing more
Painfully growing but fine
I'm dancing with the hand of time

One step ahead
Not sharing my bed just yet
That's as honest as I can get
But slowly my heart's making room
And real change is coming soon

I'm on the other side of last year
In a different headspace
In a "been there, now I'm here" place
Ready to let someone catch my eye
Leaving the past that I held so dear
'Cause I'm on the other side of last year

Disappointment is not forever
And any more I know I can weather

I'm on the other side of last year
In a different headspace
In a "been there, now I'm here" place
Willing to chance another goodbye
I'm stronger than my greatest fear
'Cause I'm on the other side of last year

Perfect Silence

You stole my heart first
And I had nothing left to say
I was robbed of my words
When you took my breath away
I was rendered speechless
By something I never knew
And in that perfect silence
I fell in love with you

My thoughts swirled about
But I let them stay unspoken
We were blessed by a sound
That wasn't meant to be broken
It was too good for words
Any more just wouldn't do
And in that perfect silence
I fell in love with you

I told myself not now
As I grew beautifully weak
'Cause our moment grew stronger
The longer I didn't speak

I fell in a sea
Of overwhelming emotion
I didn't want to leave
So I held on to the notion
That less is really more
When you know something is true
And in that perfect silence
I fell in love with you

Picks and Shovels

When the Irish came, they were here to stay
Many raised a family on two dollars a day
They faced starvation and rampant disease
But the Brooklyn Bridge was their masterpiece

They cleared the mud and the boulders away
Back breaking work every hour all day
They used their brains along with their muscles
To build a new world with picks and shovels

They wore dirty boots and were always dirt poor
But their Irish roots wanted something much more
They were willing to dig through stress and strife
Just for the chance to live a better life

They were jeered by some as the low of the low
Called drunkards and thieves and mindfully slow
Desperate to rise from their shanty town hovels
They carried a dream with their picks and shovels

These soulful "Sandhogs", cursed with damnation
Lived through hell to build a new foundation
And I'm sure they lacked enough bread and cheese
But their sacrifice was their masterpiece

They cleared the mud and the boulders away
Went underwater to where the bedrock lay
They used their brawn to draw on their muscles
To build a new world with picks and shovels

Railroads, parks, tunnels, and streets
Their handiwork lies everywhere at our feet
And I'm sure Saint Paddy is raising his glass
To all the lads that once busted their ass

How can you pay such a timeless debt
To those mighty hearts that you never met
Huddled together on the Lower East Side
They carved out our future one day at a time

To think of them now, I am humbled at best
Their "lives on the line" puts mine to the test
For O'Malley and the likes of his friend "Red" Russell
They carried a dream with their picks and shovels

From bare existence they rose from their hovels
And it took a lot more than picks and shovels

Refused

I repeated my story I got a raw deal
I got off on how righteous it made me feel
I ran that tape around in my head
Couldn't see inside my heart lying dead

For the longest time I refused to forgive
And that's done me more harm than you ever did

Couldn't stop the blame, couldn't stop the pain
Just confused the two as one and the same
Couldn't stop the noise, couldn't stop the voice
That you were only good as a bad choice

I pretended what ended was no big deal
I told all my friends I would quickly heal
Call it the sickness of denial and pride
Couldn't run from feelings I hid inside

For the longest time I refused to forget
And there's nothing like hurt to foster regret

Couldn't stop the blame, couldn't stop the pain
Just confused the two as one and the same
Couldn't let it go, couldn't ever admit
Hating you didn't help me one little bit

I must've felt the weight of certain defeat
'Cause it lifted me out from under my feet

Couldn't lie anymore, couldn't run away
Couldn't live like that for another day
Finally let it go, finally had to admit
I wasn't the only one with a bone to pick

For the longest time I refused to make nice
And all that did was bury me twice

For the longest time I refused to forgive
And that's done me more harm than you ever did

Right Where You're Standing

Right where you're standing
There used to be a wall
It was made of fear and doubt
And suspicion just as tall

I tried to get around it
But every opening was closed
And you stood guard with your heart
That never got exposed

Let me go is what I heard
And you weren't moved by any words
I only wanted the love we found
But you wouldn't give an inch of ground
I pleaded for you to stay
That we'd find a way somehow
And right where your standing
Is where it all went down

The sun was clearly shining
On that solemn April day
But my face was raining tears
Knowing you would never stay

I tried to get around it
But every opening was closed
And you stood guard with your heart
That never got exposed

Let me go is what I heard
You weren't convinced this love could work
And you were right I had no power
But I am glad I do this hour
I prayed this hurt would go away
And I'd get there somehow
And right where your standing
Is where my sun is raining down

Let me go is what I say
We had a chance you gave away
I only wanted the love we found
But you wouldn't give an inch of ground
I pleaded for you to stay
That we'd find a way somehow
And right where your standing
Is where it all went down

Rule of Thumb

Yesterday it was here, today it's gone
You turn it off and you turn it on
And you expect me to just follow along
Undaunted, unfazed, and unperturbed
Well, don't confuse me with the absurd

Too many messages, all of them mixed
If you call this loving, it needs to get fixed

Rule of thumb: Don't let love linger
That's a forewarning from my forefinger
And my middle digit will speak for itself
If you don't offer me something else
And I might be wearing this pinky ring
But you haven't won much of anything
And this finger right here says baby understand
You won't just slide something on my hand
'Cause somewhere out there I can do better
Rule of thumb: Get your shit together

Everyone carries a doubt now and then
No matter how much love you think you're in
And sometimes the path is just a dead end
But a rocky road is cluttered with rocks
You need to get rid of those stumbling blocks

Too many messages, all of them mixed
If you call this loving, it needs to get fixed

Rule of thumb: Don't let love linger
I'm pointing that out with my trigger finger
And my middle digit will speak for itself
If you don't offer me something else
And I might be wearing this pinky ring
But you've never had my heart on a string
And this finger right here says baby understand
You won't just slip something on my hand
'Cause somewhere out there I can do better
Rule of thumb: Get yourself together

You're in, you're out, you're up you're down
And all we're doing is losing ground

Rule of thumb: Don't let love linger
That's a forewarning from my forefinger
And my middle digit will speak for itself
If you don't offer me something else
And I might be wearing this pinky ring
But you haven't proved you're the real thing
And this finger right here says baby understand
You won't just slide something on my hand
'Cause somewhere out there I can do better
Rule of thumb: Get your shit together

SEE YOURSELF

See yourself as strong
Like the angels in you do
They see that real fierceness
That I've always seen in you
Stand tall and walk the path
That is made for no one else
Embrace every moment
And the beauty of yourself

See that shining star
Your place in the world
Grab a hold of that vision
And don't be shy little girl
Dream big and beautiful
And see the journey through
Beyond the shadowlands
The sun will follow you

See yourself always
As progress in the making
Give everything you've got
And know what you're taking
Reach around the corner
Down a hidden avenue
Beyond your comfort zone
You can learn a thing or two

See that shining star
Your place in the world
Grab a hold of that vision
And don't be shy little girl
Dream big and beautiful
And see the journey through
Beyond the shadowlands
The sun will follow you

See yourself as good
'Cause that's what you're about
Fill your heart with tenderness
Whenever you're in doubt
And find the will to speak
When you think you've lost your voice
And don't forget to laugh
When there is no other choice

See that shining star
Your place in the world
Grab a hold of that vision
And don't be shy little girl
Dream big and beautiful
And see the journey through
Beyond the shadowlands
The sun will follow you

SHE RUNS REALLY WELL

She runs around and breaks my heart
She even runs up my credit cards
She runs me ragged and I'm a rambling wreck
She's like a pain that runs down my neck

She runs the risk of making things worse
'Cause she always knows how to run-in reverse
She runs me over when I'm under her spell
Yeah, she's like my car, she runs really well

She can run hot and she can run cold
She runs here and there so nothing takes hold
She runs for the hills when trouble gets thick
And runs back to me on the double quick

She runs the risk of making things worse
'Cause she always knows how to run-in reverse
She runs me over when I'm under her spell
Yeah, she's like my car, she runs really well

She can run sweet, but she can run bitter
She runs her mouth on what used to be Twitter
If any haters out there run into her
I would run for cover 'cause she's good for her word

She runs the risk of making things worse
But she'll never run when her pride comes first
She'll run you in circles like a bat out of hell
'Cause she runs the show that she knows so well

I can't really say she runs with the best
But if there's better than her, run your own test
She'll run away with your heart and run up the bill
But nothing about her is run-of-the-mill

She runs me over when I'm under her spell
Yeah, she's like my car, she runs really well

She Still Loves Her Shoes

She says they fit like a glove, gives her sole a lot of love
So, it seems I can't compete with the comfort on her feet

I've done everything I can to be the perfect man
But no matter what I do, she still loves her shoes

I mean she's really unlike anyone I've ever known
She doesn't take them off as soon as she gets home

It's like cheating in the open and flaunting an affair
But this time it's with something she only wants to wear

Platforms, Mary Janes, and someone named d'Orsay
Slingback, T-Straps, and White Ballerina Flats
Peep Toe, Stiletto, and don't forget the Pumps
Now you know why I'm so down in the dumps

When her arches start to hurt, I try to get there first
'Cause I think I'm just as sweet as what she slips on her feet

It's just a little fetish, and I know it's all sincere
But sometimes in the bedroom it gets a little weird

Scarpin, Moccasin, Low Crocs, and High Tops
Oxford, Chunky and that real Kitten Heel
Thigh High, Desert, and every kind of boot
Cowboy, Army and it comes with a salute

I've done everything I can to be the perfect man
But no matter what I do, she still loves her shoes

Docksides, Slip-Ons, and there's even Lobster Claw
I mean give a guy a break and someone pass a law

I've done everything I can to be the perfect man
But no matter what I do, she still loves her shoes

She Won't Be Me

I've heard all this before
And I left an open door
So I wish that you had more
To really offer me
It appears the words you swore
Were just lies and nothing more
So I hope you find amour
But baby without me

I'm sure it will be better
Than what we had together
It may even last forever
So baby, set yourself free
Just a friendly reminder
When you do wine and dine her
I know nothing will be finer
'Cause darling, she won't be me

The sin is with the sinner
And you were no beginner
Through thick and thin got thinner
Baby, time to confess
You put me through the ringer
So here's my middle finger
Want my memory to linger
Before we say God bless

I'm sure it will be better
When you find your new forever
You'll be so happy together
So baby, set yourself free
Just a friendly reminder
When you do wine and dine her
I know nothing will be finer
'Cause darling, she won't be me

Wouldn't want to tread on your happiness
So let's say goodbye to this lovely mess

I'm sure it will be better
When you find your new forever
You'll be so happy together
So baby, set yourself free
Just a friendly reminder
When you do wine and dine her
I know nothing will be finer
'Cause darling, she won't be me

Somebody Lied

Kiss a frog and you get a prince
Wish on a star and dreams come true
State your affirmations clearly enough
And love will find you right out of the blue

Somebody lied and I want their name
Someone to yell at, someone to blame
Who's ever out there pulling the strings
Hasn't pushed me closer to the real thing

'Cause I'd like to find my soul mate
Before my expiration date
Kiss a frog and you get a prince
Somebody lied and they've been lying since

Fate is busy helping someone else
'Cause God helps those who help themselves
Well, that's defamation if you ask me
I followed the rules and here's what I see

Somebody lied and is playing a game
All those fairytales don't end the same
Did Wendy fly off with Peter Pan
And did Lois Lane marry Superman

'Cause I'd like to find my soul mate
Before my expiration date
Fate is busy really makes me wince
Somebody lied and they've been lying since

All those stories that have manifested
Have never really been time-tested

Somebody lied about how love goes
It's always the myth that takes control
And I'm a little pissed to say the least
I'm still a Beauty without my Beast

'Cause I'd like to find my soul mate
Before my expiration date
Kiss a frog and you get a prince
Not if the toad is a guy named Vince

Kiss a frog and you get a prince
Somebody lied and they've been lying since

Sounds Like Something You'd Say

You claim you gave me your very all
And you were in it for the long haul
And I stole your heart in my Chevrolet
Yeah, that sounds like something you'd say

I mean, c'mon
What a crazy lie
It was a Dodge Dart Sedan
And your heart was fine
'Cause you know damn well
I was your nightly feast
And if walls can talk
So can my car seats

You swear to anyone who will listen
I was the cause of what was missing
And I left you stranded on a rainy day
Yeah, that sounds like something you'd say

I mean, c'mon
How insincere
It was eighty-five degrees
And the skies were clear
And you know damn well
The stars shone bright
And if clouds could talk
They took off that night

Oh, you have your memories and I have mine
And it seems nothing changes over time

'Cause you made the point just yesterday
I was never your type anyway
And you think I might be slightly gay
Yeah, that sounds like something you'd say

I mean, c'mon
What a crock of shit
You knew our bodies
Were a perfect fit
And you know damn well
We were hot and heavy
And if walls could talk
We were twenty-four ready

'Cause you used to whisper "any night or day"
And I swear to God, you said it that way
And you can be sure those weren't my words
'Cause that sounds like something you'd say

STRINGS

On the ancient cobblestone streets of France
I saw a puppeteer making his wooden boy dance
And a woman looked on completely entranced
And I caught what she thought simply by chance

She said, "Hello little man," with a curious smile
Have you ever cut loose from those strings for a while
When you're back in your box and all locked down
Do you ever get restless and just want to break out

You see you and I are no different than some
I've got strings of my own that I dangle from
There's a hand over me like the one over you
And the strings attached are more than a few

The one on my heart sometimes cries and begs
The rest of the threads touch my arms and legs
They're hidden on me but they're not hard to see
And I know you know exactly what I mean

'Cause it's not always easy to untie a knot
When it holds together everything you've got
Just try to untangle a ball made of strings
The harder you try the more mess it brings

Yet, I'm so glad that we finally have met
You have opened my eyes monsieur marionette
And as I walk away down this boulevard
I'll reflect on our talk and unravel my heart

You see you and I are no different than some
I've got strings of my own that I dangle from
There's a hand over me like the one over you
And the strings attached are more than a few

Sweet Sue Anonymous

She had diamond eyes
And a killer smile
To be perfectly frank
It had been quite a while
She was hot and it was cold
In late December
Now I'm in a group
A full-fledged member

SWEET SUE ANONYMOUS
IS WHAT WE CALL OURSELVES
WE'RE ALL TRYING TO RECOVER
FROM A LOVE LIFE OF HELL
SHE CHEATED ON US ALL
AND WE STILL DON'T KNOW WHAT FOR
WE'RE SWEET SUE ANONYMOUS
ANOTHER VICTIM'S AT THE DOOR

He's walking in slowly
With that look I had
What the hell happened
That it turned out so bad
I said man you're not alone
Tell us from the start
'Cause we're here to help
You're very broken heart

SWEET SUE ANONYMOUS
IS WHAT WE CALL OURSELVES
WE'RE ALL TRYING TO RECOVER
FROM A LOVE LIFE OF HELL
SHE CHEATED ON US ALL
AND WE STILL DON'T KNOW WHAT FOR
WE'RE SWEET SUE ANONYMOUS
ANOTHER VICTIM'S AT THE DOOR

Just sign in at the table
And take a seat if you're able

SWEET SUE ANONYMOUS
IS WHAT WE CALL OURSELVES
WE'RE ALL TRYING TO RECOVER
FROM A LOVE LIFE OF HELL
SHE CHEATED ON US ALL
AND WE STILL DON'T KNOW WHAT FOR
WE'RE SWEET SUE ANONYMOUS
ANOTHER VICTIM'S AT THE DOOR

The Follow-Up Voice

An idea inspires
And we have a choice
Do we follow our heart
Or the follow-up voice

The one that tells you, you're less than you are
With what you possess, you'll never get far
Others have tried and most never succeed
Pick something else that is more your speed

We fall madly in love
And we have a choice
Do we follow our heart
Or the follow-up voice

The one that whispers, here we go again
I can tell you right now how this will end
Love does a number on someone's mind
It seldom lives up to humble and kind

A dream killer, an unfulfiller, a cacophony of noise
But there's another choice than the follow-up voice

The one that tells you, you're more than enough
You've got the right gifts, now share them with us
Strangers out there will offer their help
Today is your day to bet on yourself

The one that tells you, go after your dream
As long as you try, keep doing your thing
And whether love lasts forever after
You'll know it was there in every chapter

An idea inspires
We fall madly in love
Or maybe get a feeling
We know something is up
What do we do
When we have a choice
Do we follow our heart
Or the follow-up voice

THE WIND

I love to feel the wind
I love how it swirls
Like a magical dance
That suddenly unfurls

I love the wind at my back
Pushing me along
Giving me direction
To where my heart belongs

I love a tunnel of wind
That I have to fight
Challenging the elements
With all of my might

I love to hear the wind
When it rustles the leaves
I watch it grow stronger
As it flies through the trees

I try to outrun the wind
Like it's real life or death
Then I pretend to collapse
From running out of breath

I love to catch the wind
As Donovan would say
Which I know I can't do
But I try anyway

I love the wind on my face
Like a healing massage
It wakes up my senses
From any camouflage

I am jealous of the wind
And how it changes course
It goes where it wishes
With a triumphant force

I want to flow like the wind
And be as light as air
Then I know I can go
With the wind anywhere

There'll Always Be Another Josh

You know your friend has a serious crush
On the guy you're looking at way too much
Better you hug your side of the road
So you don't violate the girl code

You know first come first serve
Only one to a customer
So, play it nice and don't think twice
Keep your hands off the merchandise

Don't cheat and butt in line
Just wait your turn and do what's right
Cross your heart and take the loss
There'll always be another Josh

When he passes by with that killer smile
Just say "hey" and walk the other way
Don't stop and talk don't stop and chat
You'll be dead in the water if you do that

Be a true BFF
She was for you remember Jeff
So, play it nice and don't think twice
Keep your hands off the merchandise

Don't cheat and butt in line
Just wait your turn and do what's right
Cross your heart and take the loss
There'll always be another Josh

Keep that vow between us girls
That reverberates around the world

Be a true BFF
She was for you remember Jeff
So, play it nice and don't think twice
Keep your hands off the merchandise

Don't cheat and butt in line
Just wait your turn and do what's right
Cross your heart and don't just die
Go find yourself another guy

Yeah, cross your heart and take the loss
There'll always be another Josh

Third Time Is Not a Charm

We put our best heart forward
And gave it all we got
We thought with marriage number three
We had finally found that sweet spot

More understanding less demanding
Give and take and live and learn
We won't demolish, we'll just polish
And let forgiveness do its business
True believing, no one leaving
Forget the past and so much more
Well, third time is not a charm
When you can count to four

I thought we'd break our patterns
When love was on the line
But you had trouble changing yours
And I just doubled down on mine

I started reeling from that trapped feeling
My renegade didn't age
And you said honey where's the money
It was like no one had turned a page
Wishful thinking, lots of drinking
And give and take went out the door
Well, third time is not a charm
When you can count to four

I don't know why things go wrong
But this ring of mine just won't stay on

More understanding less demanding
Walk the talk and live and learn
Never demolish, shine and polish
And let forgiveness do its business
True believing, no one leaving
And I'll remember even more
The third time is not a charm
When you can count to four

True believing, no one leaving
And if you're out there keeping score
The third time is not a charm
When you can count to four

Up in Heaven

Don't have a needle in my arm
No urge to do myself harm
Not living on a desolate street
Broken bottles under my feet

I haven't made a bad decision
I'll never see another prison
I get all the help I really need
And nothing hurts and nothing bleeds
I'm never down never ever down
Up in heaven

Don't have to beg for anything
Finally free of suffering
Don't lie to family or to friends
Breaking hearts time and time again

I haven't made a bad decision
I'll never see another prison
I'm no angel yet by any means
But I still hope to earn my wings
Don't send me down, I'm much better now
Up in heaven

High as a kite has a different meaning
Someone divine told me I am beaming

I haven't made a bad decision
I'll never see another prison
I get all the help I really need
And nothing hurts and nothing bleeds
I'm more alive knowing I'll survive
Up in heaven

Don't send me down, I'm much better now
Up in heaven

VOLUNTEER

I decided to volunteer
And give my energy and time
How free it was to feel the love
Without asking for a dime
Someone needed me
And I needed them
And the selflessness around
Was humanity at its best

Everyone was all in
Hours of power from beginning to end
Lifted spirits hearts could hear it
And the sounds were like an amen
Hands too busy to think
There was too much at stake
Joined together under pressure
No one wanted to take a break

When a cause shows its worth
And gives soulfulness in return
It returns me to my true self
And I think that's true of everyone else
It may be momentary
It may just be that day
But the memory of changing lives
Will never ever burn away

Everyone was all in
Hours of power from beginning to end
Lifted spirits hearts could hear it
And the sounds were like an amen
It's do or die for some
Time is ticking away
Others that you'll never know
Only wish they could take your place

I decided to volunteer
And give my energy and time
How free it was to feel the love
Without asking for a dime
Someone needed me
And I needed them
And the selflessness around
Was humanity at its best

WE GOT BACK TOGETHER

We got back together
But not forever, just a month
And that four weeks was the longest time
I ever spent trying to reinvent
Something that never got better
So I can't really say we got back together

I mean we were in it for at least a minute
Until we pushed the buttons that had no limit
Pulled us every which way and that
It was the twilight zone as a matter of fact

We said now or never
So we jumped right in, yet again
And that one move soon proved to be
A thunderstorm that got reborn
Something that time couldn't weather
So I can't really say we got back together

Memory has a way of not forgetting
When you're right back in the wrong setting
Something new gets old real fast
And you can feel the weight of a tired past

Resentment came back
We were on the attack
Love was marked for death on every wasted breath
We dug no deeper
Sex was a sleeper
And as far as feelings they didn't come cheaper

We were birds of a feather
So we flew right there, on a dare
Well, stupid is as stupid does
And our wings got clipped sure enough
And I shipped out with ruffled feathers
So I can't really say we got back together

We were two peas in a very odd pod
Got no help from that guy named God
I can see Him now rolling his eyes
Thinking, "Boy, are they in for a big surprise"

We pulled the trigger
I mean go figure
We were just two nuts back in a rut
No deep thinking
Just two of us sinking
Into the pool of crazy fools

We got back together
Just like dumb and dumber
And that four weeks was a real bummer
I ever spent trying to reinvent
Something that never got better
So I can't really say we got back together

Where Are We

Where are we
Besides in this park
Staring at each other
Dreaming past the stars
Alone or together?
Who wants to answer first
It's time for us to talk
Though our words might hurt

We've traveled all these miles
Shared each other's heart
But I'm not really clear
Exactly where we are
I know we're sitting here
I know it's turning dark
But I'm not really clear
Exactly where we are

Where are we
I would like to know
High on a mountain
Or buried in the snow
Walking hand in hand
Or stepping further apart
I would like to know
And so would my heart

We've traveled all these miles
Shared each other's pain
But I'm not really clear
If that means we feel the same
I know we're sitting here
I know it's turning dark
But I'm not really clear
Exactly where we are

Where are we
Besides holding hands
The weight of our world
Needs a place to land
You haven't said a word
And I haven't given up
Baby, where are we
If we're not in love

Baby, where are we
If we're not in love

Why Are You Here

You came barging in like a warning from Hell
Called me a loser, a user, and other things as well
Got in my face like it was your rightful place
And told me I was greedy and way too needy

Now I look at you and I just feel sad
There is only one question I really have

Why are you here if what you say is true?
I'd be somewhere else if I were you
The clock is ticking for us every minute
I think you should know love has its limits
If you really believed you have something to fear
Then, I'll ask again, why are you here?

You're attacking me for something I'm not
I don't love someone for the things they've got
Maybe you equate yourself with all your stuff
But that doesn't make you worth very much

All those things you accuse me of being
I think maybe it's you that you are seeing

Why are you here if what you say is true?
I'm the worst thing that's ever happened to you
I'd be as far away as I could get
With someone who's a much safer bet
If you really don't trust that my heart is sincere
Then, I'll ask again, why are you here?

If putting me down makes you feel better
Then, your problems are bigger than ours together

Why are you here if what you say is true?
I'd be somewhere else if I were you
The clock is ticking for us every minute
I think you should know love has its limits
If you really just wish that I'd disappear
Then, I'll ask again, why are you here?

The clock is ticking for us every minute
I think you should know love has its limits
I have you to thank for making that clear
So, I'll ask again, why are you here?

Won't Push My Heart Around

Too much drinking crooked thinking
And a desire to be loved
I let myself be open season
Just to keep you fired up

I didn't recognize myself compromised
But I sure as hell do now
And you don't have that kind of pull
'Cause I won't push my heart around

I know exactly how it feels
When it's broken and let down
It doesn't breathe it only bleeds
And that's the part I won't allow
I won't be its worst enemy
I've done enough of that somehow
And you don't have that kind of pull
'Cause I won't push my heart around

Always charming and disarming
With a pocketful of lies
I got caught up in your double talk
When I looked into your eyes

And I lost my center and let you enter
And my world turned upside down
But you don't have that kind of pull
'Cause I won't push my heart around

It knows exactly where it's been
And today it's honor bound
It has a home, even when alone
And you can't take it from me now
I won't be its worst enemy
I've done enough of that somehow
Yeah, you don't have that kind of pull
'Cause I won't push my heart around

I must have been easy prey
'Cause pleasing you was my forte
As long as you were satisfied
I thought I'd never be denied

But in that foolish quest, our passion fest
Has all come crashing down
And you don't have that kind of pull
'Cause I won't push my heart around

I won't be my worst enemy
I've done enough of that somehow
And you don't have that kind of pull
'Cause I won't push my heart around

You Make Me Dream

It doesn't matter how I landed here
All I know is my heart's free and clear
Beating fast, out running the past
Listening and imagining

'Cause you make me dream
And you lift me up
You make me believe
Being lonely won't be us
And heartache and tears
Will take a backseat from here
And I know, tomorrow
Still remains to be seen
But you make me dream

I'm rising above any trace of fear
I won't deny myself the love that's here
Knowing you, in the way I do
I see tonight in the perfect light

'Cause you make me dream
And you make me sing
You make me believe
This is more than just a thing
In body and mind
You're no accidental find
And I know, tomorrow
Still remains to be seen
But you make me dream

Something I've wanted for so very long
I don't believe will ever be gone

'Cause you make me dream
And you make me glad
You make me believe
In something I've never had
A lover, a friend
And a lifetime to that end
And I know, tomorrow
Still remains to be seen
But you make me dream

Where heartache and tears
Are few and far between
You make me dream

About Peter Strong

Peter has always had a love for words. He used to recite Shakespeare out loud for an hour each day when he was in his early twenties. The sound of the language was music to his ears. So it was no accident he launched an acting career that spanned twenty-five years, and which included roles on the New York and LA stages, Soap Operas (notably *All My Children*), and you probably have seen his face in dozens of commercials. But in 2002 he came back to Philly, his hometown, went back to school, got a master's degree in education, and taught math for fifteen years before retiring in 2016. He really does work out of both sides of his brain. He feels blessed having two careers that he loved; now he is starting his third act and publishing his own storytelling. Without the loving support of his family and friends, this book would not exist, so he is eternally grateful. You can write to Peter at skalptr@aol.com.

www.ingramcontent.com/pod-product-compliance
Lightning Source LLC
Chambersburg PA
CBHW060656100426
42734CB00047B/1947